This book belongs to

· ·

· ·

GOOD NIGHT,
God
Bedtime
BIBLE STORIES

Cover illustrated by Jenny Wren
Stories illustrated by Iris Deppe, Giuliana Gregori, John Joven,
Xuan Le, Tiziana Longo, Madison Mastrangelo,
Laura Rigo, Luisa Uribe, and Jenny Wren
Additional illustrations by Jenny Wren

GOOD NIGHT, God Bedtime BIBLE STORIES

cottage door press

Contents

GOD Made the WORLD

Illustrated by Madison Mastrangelo

1

In the beginning, the world was dark. There was nothing—no animals, no food, no people. Just a vast emptiness. Only darkness existed. But God was there, and He had a perfect plan.

"This darkness needs light," He said. So God breathed light into the darkness and He called the light "day" and called the darkness "night."

"This is good," God said. And so it was.

Next, God separated the waters above from the waters below so that there was space between it all. "You're called the sky," He said. "This is good." And so it was.

Then the waters retreated and revealed dry ground. Lush plants and trees grew from the floor. Fresh vegetable gardens sprouted from the ground and beautiful flowers filled the air with wonderful smells. Snowy mountains and green valleys rose up from the ground. Thick, tall grasses covered meadows and fields. Deserts sprawled over hot lands and soft white snow covered miles of tundra. He called the ground "land" and called the waters "sea."

"This is all good," God said. And so it was.

Then, in the endless sky He put a bright and fiery sun during the day and a glowing moon at night. God scattered blazing stars across the night sky and gave moons to faraway planets.

"This is good," He said. And so it was.

4

Then God decided that creatures should live in the sky and in the sea. In the sky, He put birds of every kind—cawing seagulls, singing robins, and hooting owls. He filled the shallow parts of the ocean with colorful fish, playful dolphins, and vibrant coral. Upon the mysterious depths of the ocean floor, God formed glowing sea creatures and bright jellyfish.

"These are good," God said. And they were.

Just like in the sky and ocean, God also put creatures to live on land—creatures that could run and gallop, skitter and crawl. He made cheetahs to run, lions to roar, monkeys to play, and frogs to hop. He called these beautiful creatures "animals."

"These are good," He said. And they were.

God Made People

Illustrated by Madison Mastrangelo

"I need to create someone to care for the amazing creatures I have made," God said on the sixth day.

So He made the most beautiful creature of all — a human. God named this human Adam. "You, my son, are good," God said. And he was.

Adam lived in a place called the Garden of Eden among racing rivers and colorful gardens. God loved Adam, so He made him ruler of all living things. Adam spent his days caring for the animals and living in harmony with the creatures of the earth. Everything was good. Except there was still one thing missing.

"You need a companion," God said to Adam. So God made Eve and she became Adam's best friend. God looked at his work and smiled. It had taken Him six long days to complete this wonderful new world, so on the seventh day, He rested.

Adam and Eve loved the home God had given them. It was the most beautiful place you could imagine, full of sweet smelling plants and flowers. Sparkling streams bubbled up from the ground, and every tree was covered with delicious fruit. They didn't want or need anything because they had everything. They didn't feel fear, jealousy, or hate. There was only love. They were the happiest they could be, living with God, and among the creatures He created.

Noah's ARK

Illustrated by Iris Deppe

11

Once there was a good man named Noah who loved God and always did what He wanted. But the people around Noah were making bad decisions and hurting one another. This made God terribly sad.

"This world I've created is no longer beautiful. Everything has gone wrong," God said to Noah. "I'm going to send a flood over the earth to wash away all the evil and start over. And you can help me."

"I'll do anything you ask," Noah said.

So God told Noah to build an ark — a huge, wooden ship that would float across the earth during the flood. "Bring your family with you onto the ark so they are safe," God said. "You've been good while others have not. I will save you and your family because of it."

Next God said, "Take two of every kind of animal there is — one male and one female. Keep them safe in the ark with you." So in went the lions, zebras, and giraffes. In went the birds, reptiles, and insects. All the animals joined Noah's family on the ark.

For days, rain poured over the earth. The ark rocked over huge waves and everything was washed away. But Noah, his family, and the animals were safe in the ark.

Finally, God calmed the waters. Noah went to a window with a dove in his hand and let the dove fly away. "If the dove returns to me," said Noah, "I'll know the water is still covering the earth because there is no place for the dove to land."

Later that evening, the dove returned to him. Noah waited seven days and sent the dove back out over the earth. This time the dove came back with an olive branch in its beak! Then God said to Noah, "The earth is now dry. The flood I sent is gone."

So Noah and his family came off the ark. One by one, the animals followed. And Noah and his family made a new home on land.

"I promise to never send a flood like this again," God told Noah. Then He put a beautiful rainbow in the sky to show His promise to Noah. Now, when a rainbow can be seen beaming across the sky, we are reminded that God always keeps His promises—just like He did with Noah.

Abraham and Sarah

Illustrated by Tiziana Longo

One of Noah's family members was a man named Abraham. He was a good person who believed in God. One day, God told Abraham to leave his home. Abraham trusted God, so he and his wife Sarah did as God said. When they found their new home, God spoke to Abraham again.

"Look around you," He said. "All this land will be yours forever. You will have as many children as there are stars in the sky."

"But how?" asked Abraham. "My wife and I are too old to have children."

"Trust me," said God. "You will have a son." Abraham knew that God always keeps His promises, so he believed what God said.

A few years later, three men visited Abraham and Sarah. And they had a message: "In nine months your wife will have a baby son."

Sarah was shocked. "I'm far too old to have a child!"

"Nothing is too hard for the Lord," one man said. The words they spoke came from God. And so, God's promise came true. Sarah gave birth to a beautiful baby boy. Abraham and Sarah were overjoyed. Abraham said, "We shall call him Isaac, which means, 'he laughs.'"

Every day, Abraham and Sarah watched Isaac grow, laughing and playing.

"One day, he will become a fine young man," said his mother, proudly. And he was.

JOSEPH'S *Colorful* COAT

Illustrated by John Joven

Once there was a man named Joseph. He had twelve brothers, but their father, Jacob, favored Joseph. And to show how much, he gave Joseph a beautiful rainbow-colored coat. But the coat made Joseph think highly of himself.

"I had a dream last night that your bales of hay were bowing down to mine," he said to his brothers. Eventually they grew tired of Joseph's attitude, so they captured and sold him to merchants without their father knowing what happened to his favorite son.

Meanwhile, the merchants sold Joseph to a man who worked for the pharaoh of Egypt. But God helped Joseph by giving him the power to interpret dreams. While Joseph was in Egypt, he told many people what their dreams meant. And all the dreams he interpreted came true.

One day, the pharaoh asked Joseph to interpret his dreams. In Pharaoh's dream seven skinny cows ate seven fat cows. In another dream, seven stacks of withered grain ate seven full heads of grain.

"God is sending you a message," Joseph said. "Your dream means that seven years of good harvest will come to Egypt and seven years of famine will follow."

Pharaoh was so impressed he put Joseph in charge during the years of the great harvest and famine. During the famine back home, Jacob told his sons to go buy food in Egypt.

When they arrived there, they didn't recognize Joseph. They bowed down to him and pleaded for food. It was just like Joseph's dream!

"Brothers — it's me, Joseph!" At first, the brothers were too shocked to speak. "This was all part of God's plan. I've been able to save many lives through this famine because He has been with me this whole time."

Pharaoh was so moved by this. "I will give you and your family the best land in all of Egypt," he said. So the brothers went home and told their father the good news. Their father was overjoyed when he saw Joseph. And they all lived in Egypt for many happy years.

The
STORY OF
Moses

Illustrated by Tiziana Longo

Years after Joseph arrived in Egypt, life became very hard for the Israelites. There was a new pharaoh, who turned the Israelites into slaves. Then Pharaoh ordered that all their baby boys be banished from Egypt.

To protect her son, one mother named Jochebed hid her baby in a basket on the riverbank of the Nile.

Pharaoh's daughter found him there. She wanted to save the baby's life, so she took him to live with her in the palace. She named him Moses and asked Jochebed to be his nurse.

She didn't know that Jochebed was Moses's real mother — it was God's plan that the boy would grow up with his mother beside him. As Moses grew up, his mother secretly told him that he was an Israelite.

One day, Moses tried to help an Israelite slave who was being treated crulely. He knew he would be punished by Pharaoh for helping an Israelite, so he ran away to live as a shepherd in the desert.

Many years later, God spoke to Moses. "I have seen how my people are suffering, and I want you to go back to Egypt. Tell Pharaoh that he must free the Israelites and let them leave Egypt."

Moses was scared to go back to Egypt, but he could not refuse God. So he went to Pharaoh and asked him to let the Israelites go. Pharaoh refused. The only way they could escape was across the Red Sea.

Moses stretched out his arms and God parted the waters so they could cross safely to the desert on the other side. But when the soldiers tried to follow them, God made the water pour down on their heads. The Israelites were free at last! God had kept His promise.

Moses *and the* TEN COMMANDMENTS

Illustrated by Laura Rigo

There was a time when the Israelites were free from Egypt, but they were still suffering because there was no food in the desert where they lived. So God made them a promise.

"I will give you meat every night and bread every day, except on the Sabbath — my day of rest," He said.

That night, a huge flock of birds appeared. They were easy to catch, so the Israelites had plenty of meat to eat. The next morning, the ground was covered with white, bread-like flakes. They appeared every morning after that and were sweet to eat. The Israelites called them "manna."

Now the Israelites had food to eat, but no water to drink. They became thirstier and thirstier under the hot, blazing sun. So Moses asked God for help.

"Find a rock at Mount Sinai," said God, "and hit it with your staff."

When Moses did as God had told him, water rushed out of the rock. Now, there was lots of cool, refreshing water for everyone to drink. The people were so happy. Together with Moses they set up camp at the foot of Mount Sinai.

Then, one day, God spoke to them again.

"I have brought you here to be my chosen people," He said. "Will you obey me?"

"We will," said the Israelites.

"Then I will give you ten special laws called commandments," said God, "which show you how to serve me and how to live together peacefully."

Two days later, thunder rumbled and lightning flashed at the top of the mountain. Together, Moses and his brother Aaron climbed the mountain. When they reached the top, God gave Moses the Ten Commandments carved on two stone tablets.

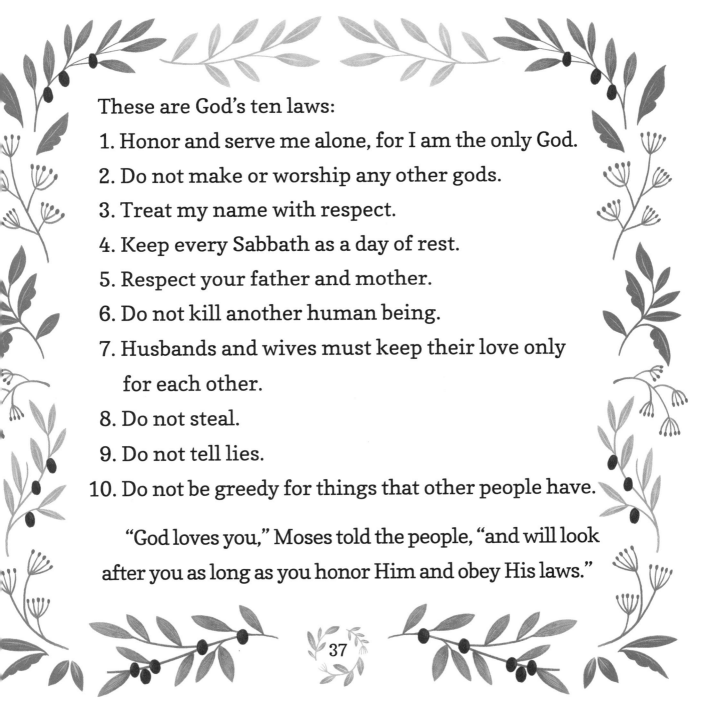

These are God's ten laws:

1. Honor and serve me alone, for I am the only God.
2. Do not make or worship any other gods.
3. Treat my name with respect.
4. Keep every Sabbath as a day of rest.
5. Respect your father and mother.
6. Do not kill another human being.
7. Husbands and wives must keep their love only for each other.
8. Do not steal.
9. Do not tell lies.
10. Do not be greedy for things that other people have.

"God loves you," Moses told the people, "and will look after you as long as you honor Him and obey His laws."

DAVID AND GOLIATH

Illustrated by Laura Rigo

39

Once there was a brave man named David who God chose to be the new king of Israel, but there were other things God needed him to do before he took the throne.

David was a shepherd. He was a great protector and used his slingshot every day to protect his father's sheep from fierce lions and bears. He was clever in other ways, too. He was famous for playing the harp, and he was asked to play for King Saul at the palace.

"Can you soothe the king with your playing?" one of the king's servants asked David. "He is in a terrible mood."

"Of course," answered David, and he began to play. Sure enough, when the king heard David's sweet music, he quickly became calmer and happier.

Far away, there was a fierce warrior named Goliath. He was ten feet tall and stronger than an ox! "Send your greatest warrior to fight me!" Goliath sneered. Only David was brave enough to take up the challenge. He knew that God would protect him.

On the day of the fight, the king offered David his own armor and sword, but David preferred to fight without it. He picked up his slingshot, put five smooth stones in his pouch, and set off to find Goliath. Goliath laughed when he saw David.

"The Israelites' greatest fighter is a boy with a slingshot!" he said. But David stood his ground.

"I come in the name of the God of Israel," he said. "I am not afraid!" David pulled one of the small stones from his pouch, put it in his slingshot, took aim, and fired.

The stone hit Goliath right between the eyes, making him lose his balance and fall to the ground. David had won!

Years later, David became the new king. His greatest legacy is teaching others that it's the size of your heart that counts. David was smaller than Goliath in physical size. But his heart, courage, and commitment to God were bigger, and that's what matters.

THE STORY OF

Ruth

Illustrated by Jenny Wren

There came a time when Israel suffered a terrible famine. Soon, many people were starving, including a man named Elimelech who lived in Bethlehem with his wife Naomi and their two sons.

"We must move to the land of Moab until the famine is over," Elimelech told his family. So they left their home behind. While they were living in Moab, Elimelech died, but his sons grew up there and married two Moabite girls, Orpah and Ruth. Some years later, both the sons died, too. Naomi was very sad.

"The time has come for me to return home," she said. Orpah and Ruth decided to go with her, but when they reached Moab's border Naomi turned to them.

"Go back," she urged. "You belong with your own people." Reluctantly, Orpah agreed, but Ruth refused.

"I'm coming with you," she told Naomi. "From now on, your people will be my people; your God will be my God."

Naomi and Ruth continued together on their journey. Ruth's company was a comfort to Naomi, but it did not stop her from worrying. How would they live without a husband to look after them? Years ago, women could not earn money on their own.

When they finally reached Bethlehem, the two women were exhausted and very hungry. Luckily, it was harvest time, and Ruth had a plan.

"Let me go out into the fields," she told Naomi. "I can pick up any grains of wheat that have been dropped. If I work hard, I can collect enough to feed us." And that's just what she did — in a field belonging to a man named Boaz.

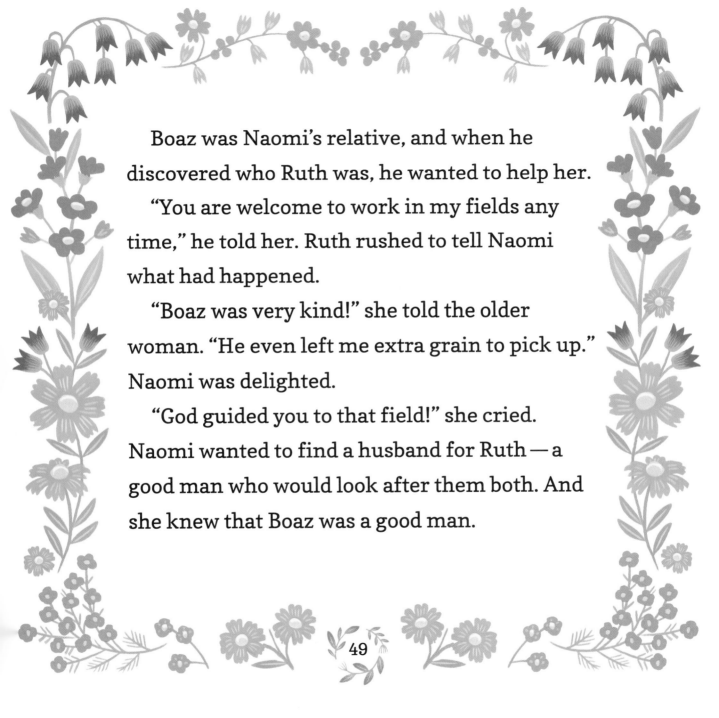

Boaz was Naomi's relative, and when he discovered who Ruth was, he wanted to help her.

"You are welcome to work in my fields any time," he told her. Ruth rushed to tell Naomi what had happened.

"Boaz was very kind!" she told the older woman. "He even left me extra grain to pick up." Naomi was delighted.

"God guided you to that field!" she cried. Naomi wanted to find a husband for Ruth — a good man who would look after them both. And she knew that Boaz was a good man.

In Israel at this time, if a man died, the closest relative would take care of his family. Naomi hoped that Boaz would live up to this, so she sent Ruth to ask for his help. Boaz was very pleased when Ruth asked for his protection. He admired her kindness to Naomi and respected how hard she worked in the fields.

"Take this gift as a mark of my respect," he said, presenting Ruth with a sack of grain. "I would very much like to marry you." And Ruth agreed. So Ruth and Boaz were married. Naomi was overjoyed, especially when Ruth gave birth to her first child. Little did anyone know then that Ruth would become the great-grandmother of Israel's greatest king — King David.

Jonah and the Big Fish

Illustrated by Xuan Le

*O*nce, in the city of Nineveh, people were making bad choices. So God called on Jonah to fix it.

"Jonah," God said. "The city of Nineveh has forgotten who I am. I want you to go there and teach people about me."

"I don't think I can," Jonah said. In fact, he was so afraid, he ran away from God. He decided to get as far from God and Nineveh as possible, so he boarded a ship to get away.

But no one can hide from God, and He knew exactly where Jonah was. The ship sailed on smooth waters. But soon, God created a storm that shook the ship! The sailors on board were scared.

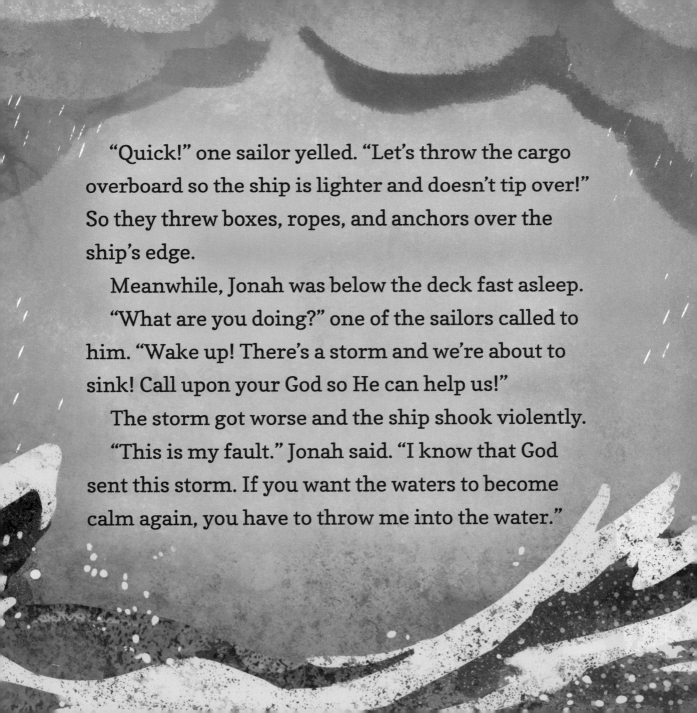

"Quick!" one sailor yelled. "Let's throw the cargo overboard so the ship is lighter and doesn't tip over!" So they threw boxes, ropes, and anchors over the ship's edge.

Meanwhile, Jonah was below the deck fast asleep.

"What are you doing?" one of the sailors called to him. "Wake up! There's a storm and we're about to sink! Call upon your God so He can help us!"

The storm got worse and the ship shook violently.

"This is my fault." Jonah said. "I know that God sent this storm. If you want the waters to become calm again, you have to throw me into the water."

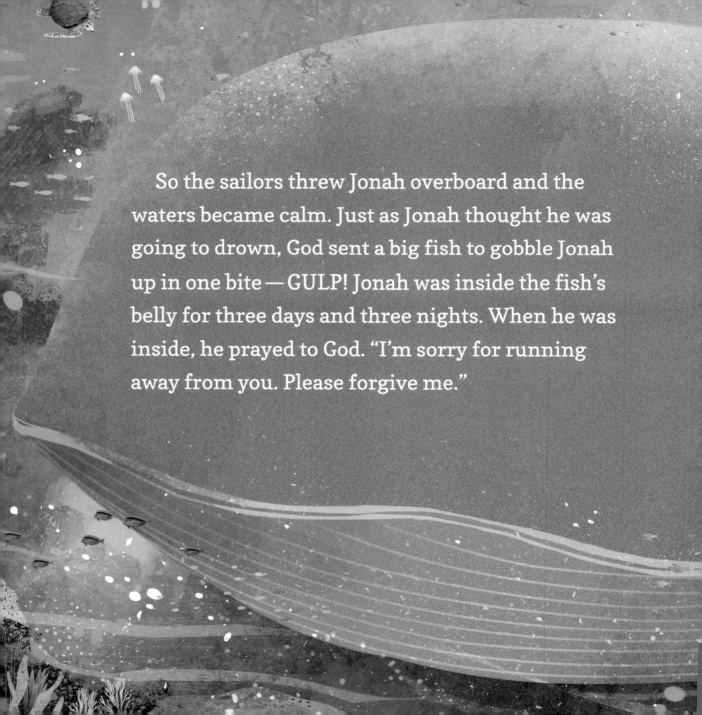

So the sailors threw Jonah overboard and the waters became calm. Just as Jonah thought he was going to drown, God sent a big fish to gobble Jonah up in one bite — GULP! Jonah was inside the fish's belly for three days and three nights. When he was inside, he prayed to God. "I'm sorry for running away from you. Please forgive me."

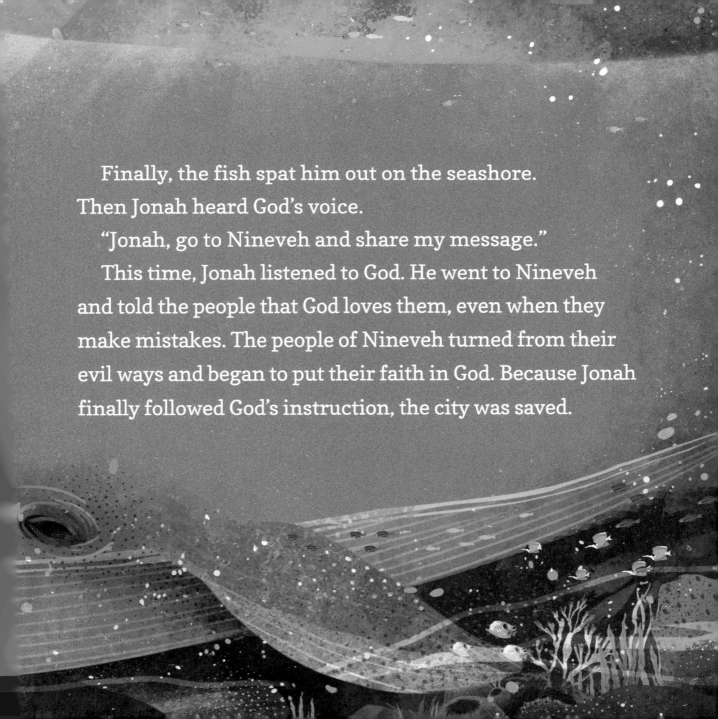

Finally, the fish spat him out on the seashore. Then Jonah heard God's voice.

"Jonah, go to Nineveh and share my message."

This time, Jonah listened to God. He went to Nineveh and told the people that God loves them, even when they make mistakes. The people of Nineveh turned from their evil ways and began to put their faith in God. Because Jonah finally followed God's instruction, the city was saved.

ESTHER BECOMES QUEEN

Illustrated by Giuliana Gregori

A beautiful young girl named Esther was among the women chosen to marry the king. Her parents were both gone, but she had been adopted by a kind, older cousin who regarded her as his own daughter. His name was Mordecai and he was a Jewish man whose family had been banished from the land.

Esther didn't tell anyone that she was Jewish because Mordecai had forbidden it. He cared about her very much and thought it would be safer if no one knew about her family background. He came to visit her every day at the palace to check how she was. Esther was liked by everyone who cared for her at the palace and she was given special treatment.

When it was time for her to meet the king, he thought she was the most beautiful woman he had ever seen. He soon fell in love with her and made her his queen.

To celebrate Esther becoming his new queen, the king gave a grand feast in her honor. He invited all his noblemen and chief officers. In addition to the magnificent banquet, he gave them all wonderful gifts and insisted that the day should be a public holiday for everyone all over the nation.

Soon after this, Esther's adopted father, Mordecai, overheard two of the guards plotting to kill the king. He went straight to Queen Esther to warn her. She passed the information on to the king. The guards were quickly arrested. Esther made sure the king knew that it was Mordecai who had passed along the information that saved him.

After this, the king loved Esther more than ever. He wanted to thank Esther. "My queen, what can I give you?" he asked. "Ask for anything, and I will say yes."

Esther gathered her courage. This was the moment for her to keep her promise to Mordecai. She hoped he would grant her request.

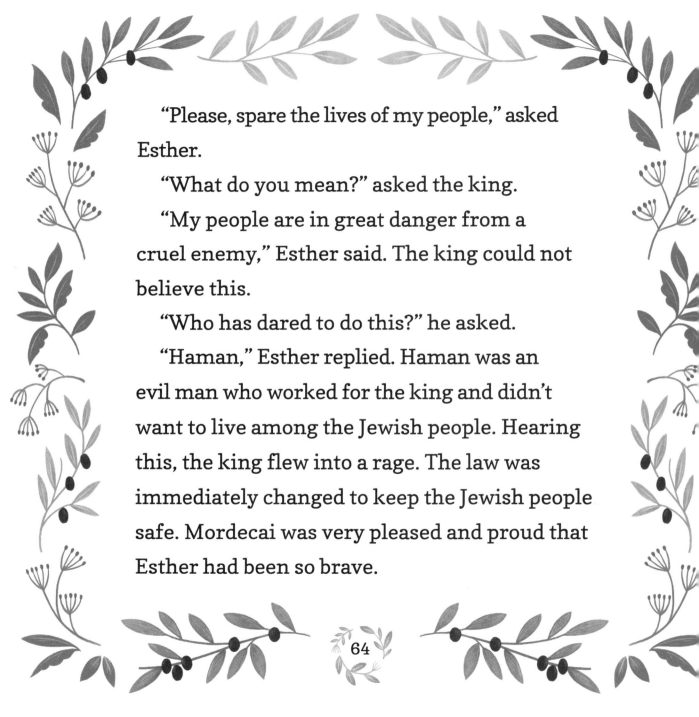

"Please, spare the lives of my people," asked Esther.

"What do you mean?" asked the king.

"My people are in great danger from a cruel enemy," Esther said. The king could not believe this.

"Who has dared to do this?" he asked.

"Haman," Esther replied. Haman was an evil man who worked for the king and didn't want to live among the Jewish people. Hearing this, the king flew into a rage. The law was immediately changed to keep the Jewish people safe. Mordecai was very pleased and proud that Esther had been so brave.

The king gave
Haman's land and
houses to Esther.
Then he called
Mordecai to the
palace and gave
him Haman's job.
Mordecai became
the second most

important man in the kingdom. He worked hard
to make sure that the people were happy and safe.
The king honored him very much, and all the Jews
loved him, too. Every year Esther's courage in saving
the lives of all her people is celebrated at the Jewish
festival of Purim.

The Birth of Jesus

Illustrated by Luisa Uribe

Once there was a woman named Mary who lived in the town of Nazareth. She was married to a man named Joseph. One day, an angel brought them news. "Mary, you will give birth to a son, and you will name Him Jesus. He will be God's son, and He will reign over everything." Mary trusted God and knew this was part of His grand plan.

Soon, God gave Mary and Joseph the greatest gift: Mary was pregnant with a baby. During this time, Mary and Joseph had to travel far away to the city of Bethlehem. While on their way, Mary suddenly knew it was time to have Him. They wanted to have the baby in a comfortable place, so they searched for an inn.

"May we have a room to stay in?" Joseph asked an innkeeper. "My wife is about to have a baby."

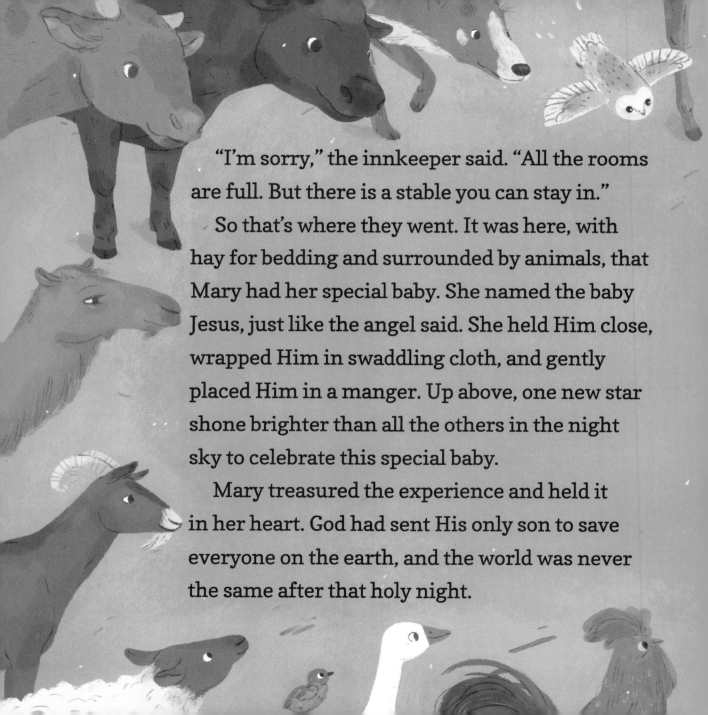

"I'm sorry," the innkeeper said. "All the rooms are full. But there is a stable you can stay in."

So that's where they went. It was here, with hay for bedding and surrounded by animals, that Mary had her special baby. She named the baby Jesus, just like the angel said. She held Him close, wrapped Him in swaddling cloth, and gently placed Him in a manger. Up above, one new star shone brighter than all the others in the night sky to celebrate this special baby.

Mary treasured the experience and held it in her heart. God had sent His only son to save everyone on the earth, and the world was never the same after that holy night.

The WISE Men and the SHEPHERDS Visit JESUS

Illustrated by Luisa Uribe

Not too far from the stable behind the inn, there were shepherds guarding their flocks. Suddenly, the night sky above the shepherds became a blaze of light, and the angel of the Lord appeared before them. The shepherds covered their eyes because they were afraid.

"Don't be frightened," said the angel. "I come with good news, which will bring great joy to the whole world. A special baby has been born in Bethlehem today. He is God's promised king — your Savior. Go and see the baby. He is sleeping in a manger."

Just then, the sky filled with angels singing, "Glory to God in the highest. Peace to everyone on Earth."

The angels disappeared, the light faded, and the sky became dark again. The shepherds knew they had not been dreaming and hurried off to Bethlehem to find the special baby: God's promised king.

The shepherds found Mary, Joseph, and their baby in Bethlehem, just as the angel had said. When they saw Jesus lying in the manger, they kneeled down to Him. The shepherds told Mary and Joseph all the things the angel had said to them as they tended their flocks earlier that night. Then they went home, praising God as they went.

The same evening, three wise men saw a bright new star in the sky. They knew that something wonderful had happened. It was a sign that a great King had been born.

So the men decided to follow the star. They took gifts with them for the special baby. They traveled for days until the star led them to a house in Bethlehem. Inside was a tiny baby. They bowed down low before Him. And the night they met Jesus was one they would never forget.

JESUS VISITS the TEMPLE

Illustrated by Tiziana Longo

When Jesus was twelve years old, Mary and Joseph took Him to Jerusalem for the Festival of Passover. The celebrations lasted a whole week. After the festival, everyone began the long journey home.

Mary and Joseph thought Jesus was traveling somewhere else in their large group. They didn't worry that they hadn't seen Him for a while, as there were plenty of other people with them. It was only when evening came and everyone met together to eat that they realized Jesus wasn't anywhere to be found.

Mary and Joseph looked for Jesus everywhere. They asked their family and friends if anyone had seen the boy. But no one had. Mary and Joseph lay awake all night worrying about their son and hoping He was safe.

As soon as daylight came, they knew they must go and look for Him. So they left the group they were traveling with and hurried back to Jerusalem. When they reached the city, they searched and searched for Him. They were so worried!

Finally, after three days, they went into the Temple. It was there that they found their son. He was calmly sitting with the men who taught God's laws. Jesus was listening to everything they said and asking questions. Everyone was amazed at how much of the teachings He understood.

Mary and Joseph were very upset. "Your father and I have been searching everywhere for you," said Mary. "We have been so worried. How could you do this to us?" Jesus was surprised they had been worried at all.

"I thought you would have known that I would be here in my Father's house," He said. Mary and Joseph didn't understand what Jesus was saying to them. But they were so pleased that He was safe. They set off for home once more, and Jesus stayed close to His parents all the way. But He never forgot the lessons He learned during His beautiful time in the Temple.

Jesus Is Baptized

Illustrated by Tiziana Longo

Just before Jesus was born, a woman gave birth to a boy named John. When John grew up, God spoke to him and said, "You will be my messenger." So that's just what John did. He told all kinds of people about God and His message of love.

"God's king is coming soon," he told them. "Tell God that you are sorry for the mistakes you've made. Change your ways, then He will forgive you."

Many people were sorry for their sins, so John led them to a river and dipped their heads underwater. This was a sign that their sins had been washed away. It was called "baptism."

"Are you God's promised king?" people asked him.

"No," said John. "I am only a messenger. Someone much greater than me is coming soon."

Then one day, Jesus came to John.

"Will you baptize me, too?" Jesus asked. John wondered how a regular man like him could baptize God's promised king.

"You should baptize me, Lord," he said, bowing to Jesus.

"No, John," said Jesus. "I want the people to see me baptized and I'd like you to do it."

So John did as Jesus asked. He laid Jesus down in the river and dipped His head underwater. Suddenly the sky opened up. A voice from Heaven said, "This is my son. I love Him and I am pleased with Him."

JESUS
Feeds
5,000 PEOPLE

Illustrated by Laura Rigo

One morning, as Jesus walked beside Lake Galilee, He saw fishermen.

"Will you take me onto the lake?" Jesus asked them. A fisherman named Simon agreed. Soon Jesus began to teach from the boat. People stopped to listen along the shore. When Jesus had finished teaching, He told Simon to row farther out and drop the fishing nets there.

"We didn't catch any fish there last night, but we will do as you ask," said Simon, and he and his brother rowed to the middle of the lake and dropped their nets. Instantly, the nets filled with fish. There were so many that Simon thought the boat might sink, so he asked nearby fishermen for help.

They knew they were watching something very special. Then Jesus said to them, "Come and follow me. From now on you will work with people, not fish." After this, Jesus called others to be His closest companions and share His work. They were called His "disciples."

As time passed, more and more people came to listen to Jesus. He would speak to the crowds for hours at a time. One day, Jesus was teaching by the lake. By sunset, 5,000 people had gathered around Him. It had been a long day, and they were all very hungry.

"Please send the people away," the disciples begged Jesus. "Tell them to walk to the farms and villages to find food."

But Jesus replied, "Why don't you give them food?"

Jesus's disciple Andrew stepped forward. "This boy is offering to share five loaves and two fish, but that won't be enough to feed this crowd," he said.

Jesus took the loaves and fish, thanked the boy, and then thanked God for this food. Then He gave the food to the disciples, who broke it up and handed it out to the people. Miraculously the amount of food doubled and tripled, and everyone ate as much as they wanted. When they had finished, the disciples gathered up twelve full baskets of leftover food. It was a miracle!

JESUS

Walks on

WATER

Illustrated by Laura Rigo

95

Jesus performed miracles. He fed, healed, and helped many people. One day, after Jesus performed a miracle in front of a large crowd, He told His disciples to go ahead of Him. "Get in the boat and go to the other side of the water and I'll meet you there soon," Jesus said. Then He went up to the mountain to pray and be alone for a while. Jesus would often spend time alone, praying for God's guidance.

That night, Jesus climbed down from the mountain and went to the seashore. He put one foot out onto the water, then another. He did not sink!

He continued to walk across the water, all the way to the disciples' boat.

The disciples were frightened when they saw Jesus walking toward them. They had never seen anyone walk on water before and thought it was a ghost. Jesus saw that they were scared and said, "There's no reason to be afraid! It's me, Jesus."

Peter said, "If you are who you say you are, ask me to walk on the water toward you."

"Come out and walk to me, Peter," said Jesus. So Peter placed one foot on the surface of the water, then another. Peter was walking on water, too! Suddenly, a big gust of wind blew and Peter became frightened. He started to sink!

"Lord, please help me!" Peter cried.

Jesus took Peter's hand and brought him back to the surface of the water. "You didn't have much faith walking across the water. As soon as the winds blew, you doubted me," Jesus said.

Then Jesus and Peter climbed back into the boat and the winds and water became still. Everyone had faith in Jesus again and said, "You are the true Son of God!"

When they finally got back on land, a large crowd flocked to Jesus. They brought people who were sick and suffering to Jesus so He could make them feel well again. For they knew if they touched even the fringe of His cloak they would be healed. And they were.

JESUS
Blesses the
CHILDREN

Illustrated by Giuliana Gregori

101

Many people thought Jesus was so wonderful, and so they brought their children to meet Him. They wanted their children to be near Him so He could pray for them and bless them.

One day, a crowd of parents and children arrived on a hill where Jesus was teaching. Jesus's disciples saw them coming and yelled at them for bothering Jesus.

"Leave Jesus alone," they said. "He's been teaching all day. He's tired and He needs to rest." Even though His disciples were just trying to help Jesus, He asked them to stop yelling at the parents of the children.

"Let the little children come to me," He said. "Don't stop them. The Kingdom of God belongs to people like them. This is the truth: anyone who wants to enter the Kingdom of God must learn how to while they're little."

Then He called the children to Him. Jesus knew it was important to spread the word of God and His love to these children. If they learned about God and His message early on, they would carry His love with them in their hearts for their entire lives.

The happy parents brought their children forward to Jesus. He took the children in His arms, welcomed them all, and blessed them. He spoke to them of God's love and His kingdom. The little children listened closely and promised they would keep God close to their hearts and in their mind as they grew up. They promised to be kind, just like Jesus.

Jesus

ENTERS

Jerusalem

Illustrated by Xuan Le

The streets of Jerusalem were full of people getting ready to celebrate the Passover festival. A little way outside the city, Jesus arrived at the Mount of Olives. He spoke to two of His disciples.

"Go to the village ahead," He said. "As you enter it, you will find a young donkey tied up. No one has ever sat on it. Bring the donkey to me. If anyone asks you what you are doing, say that I have told you to do this, and I will return the donkey soon."

The disciples walked into the village. Soon they saw the donkey tied up just as Jesus had said. As they were untying the donkey, some people spoke to them.

"What are you doing?" they asked. The disciples told them what Jesus had said, and the people let them take the donkey to Him.

When the people in Jerusalem heard that Jesus was coming to the city, they hurried to meet Him. Some of them threw down their cloaks on the road in front of Him. Others cut palm branches from the trees and laid them down before Him. Crowds gathered around Jesus shouting words of praise.

"Hosanna!" they shouted. "God's promised king is coming!"

"It is Jesus!" shouted the happy crowds. "The prophet from Nazareth." Everyone cheered as Jesus rode into the city like a king.

Once Jesus arrived in Jerusalem, he went straight to the Temple. But when He got there, He couldn't believe what was happening. People were treating the Temple like a market. They were buying and selling things there, instead of praying to God. Jesus looked around at the people in the Temple. There were men exchanging money for special Temple coins. There were other men buying and selling doves. Jesus was shocked.

"This is God's house," He said. "It is supposed to be a place of prayer." From that moment on, He would not allow anyone to buy and sell at the Temple. Jesus started to teach there every day. Sick people came to Him to be cured. People were amazed by Him and His love.

The
EASTER
Story

Illustrated by Xuan Le

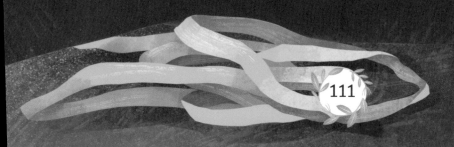

111

Jesus was always kind. He healed the sick, fed the hungry, and gave to the poor. He showed God's love to everyone. Even still, there were people who didn't like Jesus. Leaders were jealous of Him and didn't like Jesus's teachings. They were so angry that they wanted Jesus gone.

The time was coming for Jesus to leave the earth, so Jesus and His twelve disciples had one last meal together. During the Last Supper, Jesus told His disciples to remember Him each time they broke bread and drank wine together.

"It's time for me to leave this earth," said Jesus. "This is all part of God's plan. But I will come back to you in a glorious way."

Soon after, Jesus went outside to pray to God. He was afraid of what was to come, so He knelt down and asked for strength.

"God, I am ready to give up my life so that others can live. I know this is Your will for me: to die so that everyone on Earth may be saved."

When He got up, the angry leaders arrested Jesus and took Him away. They placed Jesus on the cross. Everyone who loved Jesus was very sad and wept for Him. Even in the sadness, God was still at work. He had one more miracle to reveal.

After Jesus died, a man wrapped Jesus's body in cloth and laid Him in a tomb. Then he rolled a big stone over the tomb's entrance so no one could get in. Three days later, three women went early in the morning to visit Jesus's body. When they arrived at the tomb, the heavy stone had been rolled away. When they went into the tomb, Jesus's body was gone!

Just then, two men appeared. They said, "Jesus isn't here — He has Risen! What He said was true: He would die and rise again to be with God in Heaven. Go and tell the disciples this great news!"

The two women went back to the disciples to tell them the great news that Jesus was alive! Later, Jesus went to be with His disciples. The disciples were so surprised to see Jesus alive.

"Touch my hands and feet to see that I am alive and it is me." So the disciples touched Jesus's hands and believed. They shouted with joy. Then Jesus gave them specific instructions.

"You are to spread the good news about me to all people. God's plan has been fulfilled; I have died for everyone's sins so that they can live life to the fullest." Then Jesus left the earth to be with God in Heaven.

The miracle of Jesus rising from the grave is celebrated on Easter Sunday. Christ has Risen! Hallelujah!

Look After My Family

God bless Mom and Dad
For all the good times we have had;

For vacations, birthdays,
    Christmas fun;
For games and races that I won!

For afternoons spent in the park;
For watching fireworks after dark;

For all the stories they have read
At night, when I go to bed.

Keep them safe, oh God, I pray,
So I can love them every day.

Help Me to Be Good

Dear God,
Help me to be good
When I have to share my toys.
Help me to be good
When I'm making too much noise.

Help me to be good
And eat up all my greens.
Help me to be good
When I'm tempted to be mean.

Help me to be good
Each and every day.
Help me to be good
In every single way.

Now I Lay Me Down to Sleep

Now I lay me
down to sleep,
I pray, dear God,
my soul to keep.

Your love to guard me
through the night,
And wake me with
the morning light.

Time to Sleep

It's time to sleep.
I've brushed my teeth and read my book,
I've put my robe on the hook, and...

I just can't sleep.
The bed's too hot, the light's too bright,
there's far too many sounds tonight, but...

I still can't sleep.
I've shut my eyes, I've said a prayer,
"God bless children everywhere," then...

Perhaps I'll sleep.
I think I might. I think I'll — yawn —
turn out the light.
Goodnight.
Zzzzz...